MERIDIAN
MEDITATION

MERIDIAN MEDITATION

Your Guide to Achieving True Holistic Meditation

MICHAEL MINGCAI ZHAO

To order additional copies of this book, contact:
Xlibris LLC
1-888-795-4274
www.Xlibris.com
Orders@Xlibris.com
686778

CONTENTS

PREFACE

TODAY MANY PEOPLE ARE suffering. People are suffering physically and psychologically more than ever before. There are many factors that contribute to this—with financial pressures and work being the most widespread. People have to work harder to have the things they desire and, sometimes, just to make ends meet. Often people do not actually enjoy the work they are doing and simply do it out of necessity. They have no peace of mind, and they do not have the ability or the time to enjoy life; this usually generates a large amount of stress and, as a result, diseases. These diseases are another major contributor to the constant suffering we see—whether from stress or the toxins in our food—and they usually lead to the consumption of medications. Mainstream medicine, however, only seems to treat the symptoms and does not get to the root cause, so those suffering will often continue to suffer. Though acupuncture and Chinese herbal medicine can help, a lack of recognition by the medical industry and Canadian government makes it impossible for those seeking alternative medical treatment to receive their treatments free. Individuals who purchase health benefits or receive benefits through their employer have a very limited amount of funds that their insurance will allocate to acupuncture in comparison with other more widely recognized alternative health practices (ex. physiotherapy and chiropractic sessions). As a result, acupuncture and similar alternative health practices have less of a reach and cannot do much to help those who could benefit from it.

In China, I studied both alternative and Western medicine for over eight years and have practiced both for fourteen years. I have practiced alternative medicine in Canada for over sixteen years. In all my experience, I have found that Meridian Meditation, originating in China, is a great way to help alleviate the physical and psychological issues that plague so many people today.

Meridian Meditation treats almost all diseases better than mainstream medicine, and can even treat some diseases better than acupuncture and Chinese herbal medicine. This is because these medical practices cannot successfully treat every issue. With modern medicine, prescription drugs force the body to rely on them by weakening the body's systems. Acupuncture does not have the ability to correct energy deficiencies, which can lead to diseases such as chronic fatigue syndrome and can lower energy stores even further if used. It is often difficult for Chinese herbal medicine practitioners to diagnose and correct deficiencies, and if misdiagnosed, this can make the issue worse. This is why Meridian Meditation is a very effective treatment for most, if not all, diseases—it is 100 percent natural and completely free of long-lasting side effects. Meridian Meditation utilizes your body's natural healing capabilities, allowing your body to target and heal what ails you accurately and efficiently.

For many years, I suffered from colitis and both stomach and duodenum ulcers, and in 1979, I began to study medicine in the hopes that I could figure out how to cure myself. When I was attending medical school, I visited many of the best doctors in my area—both Western and alternative health practitioners—and they were unable to help me. As my symptoms worsened, I finally made the decision to take a year off from school. During my time off, I began to study Meridian Meditation, and after a short time, I began to feel better. I have lived in Canada for over sixteen years now, and other than a few physical checkups, I have not had to see a doctor at all. This is how effective Meridian Meditation can be. I have recommended Meridian Meditation to some of my clients, usually at the beginner or intermediate I level, and it has greatly improved their health.

Meridian Meditation has been practiced in China for over 3,500 years, but it is a slow process. In a society where everyone is looking for and has the ability to receive a quick fix, most have not developed the patience and focus necessary to receive the wonderful benefits Meridian Meditation can provide. Other similar practices, like yoga, have become more of a physical activity, but this is not the case with Meridian Meditation. This Meditation differs from other mind/body practices because it helps to integrate the mind, body, and soul, utilizing the mind to shift energy within the meridians to bring about healing. Meridian Meditation can take you out of your state of suffering and provide you with incredible health, youthful vitality, and even build a base to help you develop superhuman abilities! This book is to help those who are interested in taking control of, and caring for, their own well-being and improving their health. Using Meridian Meditation requires patience and an open mind.

THE MAIN CAUSES
OF DISEASE

THE BRAIN IS CONSTANTLY being overstimulated by TV and electronics, and this overstimulation causes uneven distribution of the body's energy stores. When the brain is overstimulated and constantly being utilized, there is not enough energy left to regulate your system, and this can cause disconnection or separation between the mind and body. The lack of integration between the mind and body results in diseases.

Constant stress from working too hard, legal disputes, disharmonious family relations, etc. is another contributory factor to diseases. Stress is the main cause of neuro-endocrine disorder, a block of incoming information from the brain to the body's organs. With this informational block, the body's organs do not function correctly.

Today people do not go outside much and because of this they are unable to take in sunshine or spend time with nature. Outdoor activity is something that the body needs, but we are all too distracted with electronics or busy doing all the things we think we need to do to take the time to go outside. And as a result, we suffer from vitamin D deficiencies, and our bodies cannot not rid themselves of toxins through perspiration. We also have less energy flow through the meridians causing a disconnection of the mind and body.

Too much fast food and/or artificial additives in our food results in a buildup of toxic chemicals, which pollutes the internal organs, reduces energy flow, and causes a meridian block.

Health supplements are very concentrated, and if too much is ingested, it can also block the meridians and cause side effects. A high concentration of health supplements in the body can surprise some systems (ex. vitamins can cause disruption in the digestive system). Supplementation can cause an imbalance. Most people just pay attention to the ingredients, but are unaware of the nature of the supplement they are using, and so they tend to misuse these products and/or take much more than they actually need, and this action is what causes the imbalance.

Alcohol, caffeine, cigarettes, and other similar substances can fill your body with toxins and disrupt the body's natural functioning abilities. Alcohol, for example, disables your mind-body communication system. This disharmony results in a blockage in the body's natural energy flow, leading to diseases.

Medications are widely used to aide in alleviating painful and uncomfortable symptoms, to treat ailments or even as a preventative measure (ex. birth control); however, these medications are only temporary solutions, and the side effects and disruption these medications cause often leave you worse off than before you took them. Here are some examples of how these medications can negatively affect you.

- Laxatives are a common over-the-counter medication and are used to help treat constipation. When laxatives are taken, they disrupt the body's natural ability to keep you regular. Laxatives artificially push on the gut muscles to force bowel movement, and so when one chooses to use laxatives for a prolonged period, rather than more healthy alternatives like fiber and energy-increasing practices, the body is no longer able to produce bowel movements naturally.
- Sleeping pills, used to treat insomnia, causes a disconnection in the body-mind communication ability, more specifically, the communication pertaining to the maintenance of your body's internal clock. When one is unable to sleep and takes a sleeping

pill, it provides relief for a short time, but once the body gets used to the sleeping pill, those suffering with insomnia are right back where they started. Acupuncture and other alternative health methods can help prior to starting with the sleeping pill, but once sleeping pills have been used for a prolonged period, it is very hard to bridge the gap and correct the damage done. Sleeping pills also have wide variety of lasting side effects, with the most important one being that the use of sleeping pills lowers energy in the brain and disables the body's ability to properly regulate your sleep cycle. By the time tolerance to the pill is built up, the lack of ability for the mind and internal organs to communicate is so severe that the user suffers much more than when they began taking it.

- Blood pressure medication, used to treat high blood pressure, dilates the blood vessels to allow more blood to flow through the body and this, as a result, lowers blood pressure. However, the problem that caused blood pressure to rise in the first place is still within the body. Usually, blood pressure will rise when something is blocking the blood vessel (ex. blood clot) and this problem can become more severe and can spread to other parts of the body, even if blood pressure is lowered by medication. The medication also weakens blood vessels, and the constant pressure from taking the medication leads to fragility of the blood vessels. Fragility eventually causes blood vessels to break, resulting in internal bleeding and can even lead to a brain aneurysm or stroke.

- Painkillers, both over-the-counter and prescription, initially help stop pain within the body; but once the medication is fully dissolved, the user often gets rebound pain. As with sleeping pills, tolerance is built up—there is often a need to take more to get the same effect or to go up in dosage, or even switch to a stronger pain-killer. Withdrawal from strong painkillers (ex. codeine and morphine) can put users at high risk for sudden death. Long-term use of painkillers will often turn into chronic pain because painkillers lower your body's pain tolerance level and healing power significantly. Using painkillers to mask the pain does not allow for the treatment of what is actually causing the pain and so, the root cause of the pain goes untreated and may develop into something much more severe. Finally, long-term use of painkillers blocks singular flow in the meridian, which communicates with different systems within the body, causing internal disorder and severe fatigue.

- Birth-control pills are used for various reasons such as: to prevent pregnancy, reduce acne, or relieve PMS. Birth control can cause malfunctioning within the female reproductive system; birth control artificially stops normal reproductive functions and interferes with the body's hormones. Long-term use of birth control can kill communication between the hypothalamus, pituitary, and ovaries. The interference with hormone regulation within the body throws off the reproductive system, lessening one's ability to get pregnant once birth control is stopped. Again, alternative medication can sometimes help regulate the reproductive system just enough to allow for pregnancy, but it is not always able to do so in every case.

- Steroids are commonly used to reduce swelling, to temporarily relieve pain, or as an anti-inflammatory, but they rarely work for chronic pain or inflammation. Steroids suppress the immune system and disable the immune system's ability to function correctly. As a result, the immune system has poor surveillance function, which allows cells to grow abnormally. Long-term use makes serious illnesses like cancer more likely. Poor surveillance function within the immune system is closely associated with lower energy flow in the meridians. If cancer develops as a result of poor surveillance, energy within the meridians will be exhausted.

- The use of antibiotics is prevalent; but antibiotics can prevent your immune system from working correctly. Overuse of antibiotics causes your immune system to begin to rely on medication to fight off infection and bacteria. This results in the user getting sick more frequently than they did prior to taking the antibiotics. Antibiotics are meant to be used short-term and usually out of absolute necessity as using them more than necessary can make you fall ill more often. Frequent antibiotic users get sick more because this medication causes a disruption of your body's natural ability to fight off invaders.

- Chemotherapy is very toxic. It can kill off cancer cells, but it also, simultaneously, kills the cells of the immune system and other energy-making cells. Stem cells in the bone marrow are also killed because stem cells grow rapidly and this is what chemotherapy targets. Since cancer cells are being targeted and not the cause of cell mutation within the body, the cause of the disease still exists within the body, and with a damaged immune system, once treatment is over, the cancer will most likely return.

Surgery can block energy flow in the meridian. Often surgeons will target the area that is most affected (inflammation in the knee, problems with the hip or organs, infection in the tonsils), not realizing that this is merely a signal from your body that there is an issue that needs correction. Surgeons operate on the problem area, rather than the root cause, so the issue will just resurface somewhere else in the body. But that is not all! The energy flow is permanently cut off at the point of operation, so the problem will actually worsen and it will be extremely difficult to treat. Alternative health practitioners can attempt to work with this and redirect the energy, but depending on the practitioner, it is not always successful.

Brain overstimulation, stress, not enough outdoor activity, consumption of fast food consumption and food additives, overuse of health supplements, stimulants, medications (both over-the-counter and prescription), and surgery can cause poor energy, meridian blocks, body-mind separation or imbalance, and in-fighting within the body's systems. Fixing the aforementioned issues is the key to health and you can do this using these four steps:

1. Reconnecting with nature
2. Eating fresh, natural foods
3. Integration
4. Moving energy between the meridians

You can reconnect with nature by spending time surrounded by water, trees, flowers, air, sunshine, and other natural sources of energy that are beneficial to your health and this, in turn, will allow your body to detoxify itself more easily. The body can detoxify itself through the pores of your skin, through breathing, and through the release of gas from your gastrointestinal tract. Reconnecting with nature will also help calm your nervous system; the elements help stimulate the release of neurotransmitters in the brain that stabilize the nervous system. Internal organs can easily attune to nature's biorhythm, and this is essential to the body's health.

Foods need to be both fresh and natural in order to aide in improving health. Today even fruits and vegetables have additives to make them sweeter, larger or more colorful; but these additives are detrimental to your body's health as these additives are toxic. It is also essential that every meal you consume has the right ratio of proteins (like eggs, meat, and fish), vegetables, and carbohydrates (like corn, rice, and wheat) to make sure you are not getting too much of one group and not enough of the other.

The ears, eyes, nose, mouth, internal organs, skin, bones, ligaments, and limbs are all connected and part of one whole system; the meridians help each part to communicate with the other parts. The most important communications that flow through the meridians are between the brain and the body and so, any block in the energy flow will result in health issues.

When you are able to integrate and allow for some energy flow between meridians, you will be in good health, but may still experience minor illness (ex. stomach ache or flu). But when energy is able to flow freely within the meridians, you will be immune to all illnesses and it can add years to your life. When you extend your life span in this manner, the added years will be of quality as you will be in perfect health. This is why it is very important to have energy movement between meridians.

Both mainstream medicine and alternative medicine practitioners poorly recognize the importance of energy moving through the meridians and how the lack of energy movement contributes to the development of diseases. Energy flow between the meridians is needed in order to keep the body and mind connected, which corrects and prevents disease, but these practitioners rarely effectively treat this. Meridian Meditation utilizes these four steps stated previously and is a great, economical way to put these steps into action and achieve good health.

MERIDIAN MEDITATION

MERIDIAN MEDITATION IS A special practice that maximizes your ability to collect energy from various available sources and move this energy between the meridians for the purpose of achieving health and wellness and preventing disease. Meridian Meditation can heal the sick and, if practiced by those that are healthy, can help strengthen the senses, boost energy, and lead to the development of super strength.

The key elements needed to successfully achieve the health benefits Meridian Meditation can provide are: confidence, commitment, persistence, and concentration. One must have confidence and belief in Meridian Meditation in order to reap the benefits. People have a hard time believing in things that are not tangible objects, and since energy is hard to perceive, it is difficult for people to have confidence that it will help them, and so most give up after a very short period (one to two months). However, just because energy is not clearly seen, it does not mean that it does not exist. In fact, most people who are healthy are able to feel an energy boost in as little as one month. Unfortunately, most healthy people do not think it is necessary to practice Meridian Meditation, or that they will get anything out of it, but, on the contrary, healthy people are the very ones who can attain super strength and keen senses. Meridian Meditation also helps your nervous system harmonize with your body which, in turn, can gradually boost your energy. Sick people do not feel the effects as easily, and that is because their system is not functioning normally and is hardly producing enough energy to make a clear difference. The energy must first be used to help their bodies function correctly before they are able to notice any added benefits. Those suffering from mental health issues also do not see results as quickly as those that are healthy because the nervous system is afflicted and this restricts the ability for mind-body communication. Cancer patients will have to wait the longest to be able to clearly feel the benefits of Meridian Meditation as their systems are functioning poorly and any energy generated goes directly to restoring their systems, and because of this, cancer patients are usually the first to give up on the practice of Meridian Meditation.

Meridian Meditation needs to be practiced daily and requires long-term commitment. Often when Meridian Meditation is practiced, the body will begin to respond to the practice and begin to heal itself. During the healing process, you may develop some symptoms that cause discomfort. Those with colitis or Crohn's disease, for example, may experience frequent loose bowel movement or urination, but these symptoms do not mean you are getting worse—it is actually your body beginning to detoxify and heal itself. If you stay committed and continue with the practice, symptoms will soon disappear, appetite will increase, and bowel movement will be solid. For a period, healthy people may feel like something is wrong within their system, but it is simply a short-term response to the practice and this is why commitment is very important.

Meridian Meditation can boost energy in the meridians, but it must go in the correct order; and so persistence and concentration are very important. Without persistence and concentration, benefits cannot be achieved. Meridian Meditation requires the ability to shut out distraction and to focus your full attention on the meditation. However, we as a society, lack patience and focus and find it difficult to follow through with things that take an extended period.

Three things that are integral to the practice of Meridian Meditation are:

- Ability to relax and focus on specific meridian points or the energy flowing between the meridians. This is especially difficult for beginners, and those who are suffering from illness—both mental and physical—as there is a mind-body disconnection already present, but the meditation practice is important to fix this disconnect and reestablish mind-body communication.

• Deep, even stable breathing that produces no noise is necessary to the practice of Meridian Meditation. Generally, one should breathe through their nose rather than through the mouth, and breathing should be much deeper and slower than normal breathing. One should utilize their diaphragm when breathing rather than the chest. When inhaling, the stomach should expand, and when exhaling, the stomach should contract. Deep and slow breathing will draw energy in from nature and bring it down into your lower abdomen to mix with the energy brought in from other available sources. This area in the lower abdomen is referred to as the energy-synthesis field.

• Posture is very important to Meridian Meditation. Meridian Meditation can be practiced while standing, sitting or lying down, but most stand when practicing. Those who are sick usually prefer to sit or lie down. But no matter what the posture is, relaxation is extremely important.

If choosing to stand, there are two postures you can choose from:

1. You should be standing straight with feet parallel to one another and shoulder-width apart. There should be an even distribution of weight on both sides of the body. Your mouth should be relaxed, your arms should rest comfortably at your side, and your knees need to be slightly bent. Close your eyes when you begin to practice, but do not squeeze them shut! Keep your eye area relaxed (see figure 1).

Figure 1.

This figure shows standing posture 1.

2. Stand with feet shoulder-width apart. Your arms should be at your side, but with a slight distance from the body and your palms facing down. Your arms should also be slightly bent at the elbow and your knees need to be slightly bent as well. Your feet must be flat on the floor with toes curled downward (see figure 2).

Figure 2.

This figure shows standing posture 2.

If you choose to sit, begin by closing your eyes while keeping your eye area relaxed. Straighten your upper body and cross your legs, putting your hands in your lap. Make sure to overlap your hands with your palms facing up (see figure 3).

Figure 3.

This figure shows the sitting posture.

If you choose to lie down, lie on your back with your head elevated two inches and allow your body to fully relax. Your feet should be facing up, with the back of your heel resting on the bed and/or ground. Rest your hands—palms down—on your stomach. For men, the left hand should be on the stomach with the right on top; for women, the right hand should be on the stomach and the left hand overlapped on top (see figure 4).

Figure 4.

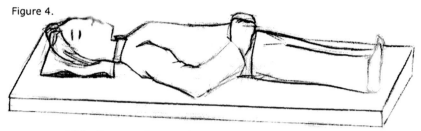

This figure shows the lying down posture.

Movement is not recommended when practicing Meridian Meditation because focusing on the energy movement within makes it more difficult.

Places in which you can practice Meridian Meditation include: mountain areas, parks, forested areas, gardens, and quiet areas near water. If you must practice indoors, you must practice by a window. It is preferable that there are trees or another source of natural energy close to or surrounding the window. Quiet is essential to the practice of Meridian Meditation and practicing in nature is the best way to achieve the relaxed state that is required, especially for beginners and those who are sick as they struggle the most with achieving a state of relaxation. The elements of nature are a source of energy and practicing Meridian Meditation in nature allows for more energy to be brought into the body, expanding the amount of energy in the meridians at faster rate.

The best times to practice Meridian Meditation are from 11:00 a.m. to 1:00 p.m., from 11:00 p.m. to 1:00 a.m. and from 3:00 a.m. to 7:00 a.m. The first reason Meridian Meditation must be practiced at these times is because the energy present in the trees, flowers, plants, and other natural elements (ex. sun, moon, and stars) are strongest at these times. The second reason is that the central nervous system is more easily calmed during these times. The third reason Meridian Meditation must be practiced at these times is that these are the times that, according to our biological clock, the internal organs are functioning best and this makes it easier for the body to collect energy. The final reason to practice Meridian Meditation at these times of the day is that the different sources of energy can mix most efficiently during these times.

THE POINTS AND
THE MERIDIANS

THE POINTS OF THE body are areas in which energy is both absorbed and released. The points are also the areas in which toxins present in the body are released. Points can be used by acupuncturists to remove blocks, increase energy flow, reduce toxins, and treat illness. Meridians are the pathways for energy flow through the different systems within the body. Meridians are only found in living organisms. Scientists have found that meridians showed low resistance and high transmission for bio-singular energy flow, and this has given people confidence in the fact that Meridian Meditation can be beneficial. Knowing the locations of the main points, and meridians on and within the body is important part of the Meridian Meditation practice.

The Locations of the Points

1. Dantian→Located within the body, at the center of the lower abdomen (see figures 5 and 6)
   - Ball-like area that serves as an energy-synthesis field.

Figure 5.

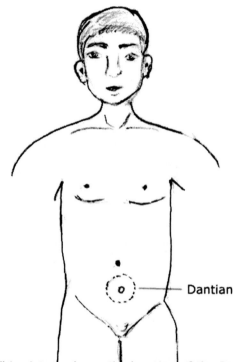

Dantian

This picture shows the location of the Dantian from a front point of view. This also shows the energy-synthesis field.

Figure 6.

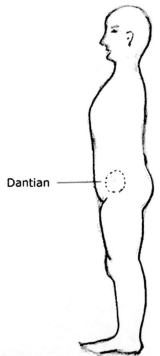

Dantian

This figure shows the location of the Dantian from a side point of view. It also shows the energy-synthesis field.

2. Mingmen or DU4→Located below the second lumbar vertebrae (see figure 18)
   - This area's point is small, about the size of the tip of a ballpoint pen.
   - This area serves as life-gate or light switch; this is where the energy goes once it is synthesized.
   - The energy located here is transferred to the Dantian area to participate in the energy-synthesis process.
   - Transfers energy through the kidneys and this energy is usually inborn.

3. Laogong or PC8→Located in the palm, between the second metacarpal bone, slightly close to the third metacarpal bone on both hands (see figure 7)
   - This area's point is also about the size of the tip of a ballpoint pen.
   - This point serves as an exchange point; this is where toxins are released and energy is absorbed.
   - When energy is absorbed from air, it is absorbed through the palms. And when toxins are released, they are released from the heart and through the palms.
   - This area serves as an exit for toxic waste from the upper body (from the waist up).

Figure 7.

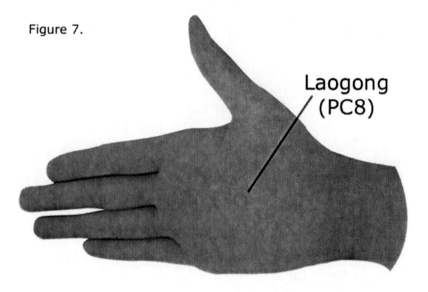

Laogong
(PC8)

4. Yongquan or KI1→Located on the soles of both feet, in between the second and third metatarsal bones (see figure 8)
   - This area serves as an absorption point for the energy that comes up through the Earth; energy from the kidneys is mainly released through this area.
   - This area also serves as a release point for toxic waste in the lower part of the body (from the waist down).

Figure 8.

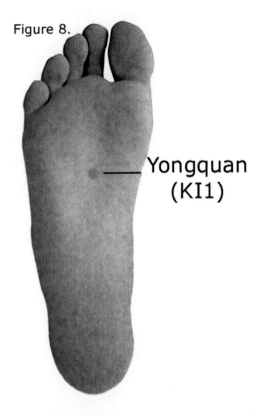

Yongquan
(KI1)

5. Baihui or DU20→Located directly at the center of the top of the head (see figure 9)
    • This area serves as a meeting and mixing point for the energy from all other meridians.
    • This area brings in energy from the sky (sun, moon, stars, etc.).
    • This area also moves all toxins released from the brain, chest, and abdomen out of the body when used together with the Laogong (PC8) and Yongquan (KI1).

Figure 9.

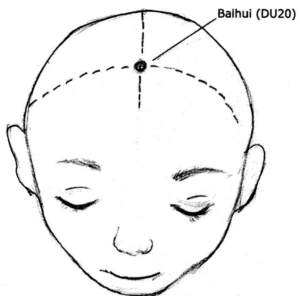

This figure shows the location of the Baihui (DU20).

6. Huiying or RN1→Located between the labia and anus in females, and scrotum and anus in males (see figure 10)
   • This area contains our body's natural energy store, the energy that is inborn.
   • This energy is sent up to the Dantian area to participate during energy-synthesis.

Figure 10.

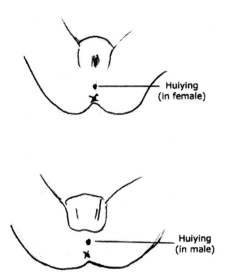

The Location of the Meridians

1. Central Axis Meridian (see figure 11)
   • Starts from Baihui or DU20, goes straight down through the chest and abdomen and ends in the Dantian.
   • When energy is being absorbed, it comes through the Baihui and ends in the Dantian. When the toxins are being released, it is first released through the Dantian and comes out through the Baihui, or it goes down through the Kidney Meridian to come out through the Yongquan (KI1). This depends on what type of practice you apply.
   • This meridian is for both collecting basic-level energy and releasing toxins if used individually or together with other meridians during energy absorption through five points. If used together with the RN and DU (see below) meridians, it can be used for boosting energy, especially when practiced at the Expert level.

Figure 11.

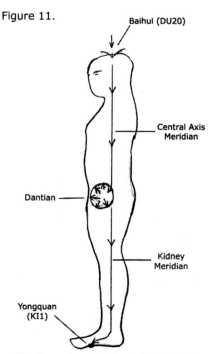

This figure shows the Central Axis Meridian.

2. Kidney Meridian or KIM (see figures 11 and 22)
   • Starts from KI1 (both right and left), moves up through the interior of the ankle, goes up through the interior of the entire leg (both right and left), through the groin area and continues up diagonally, ending in the Dantian.
   • When energy is being absorbed, it flows from KI1 through to the Dantian; if toxins are being released, it flows from the Dantian down through KI1.
   • This meridian is mainly for both collecting basic-level energy and releasing toxins when used with the Central Axis Meridian or with other meridians when practicing energy absorption through five points. When used with other meridians at the Master level, it can bring energy up to optimum levels.
3. Pericardium Meridian or PCM (see figure 19)

- Starts from the chest and obliquely ascends to the point between the underarms and shoulder, then goes down along the inside of the arm, passes the wrist area, travels through the Laogong or PC8, and ends at the middle finger.
- This meridian exists on both the left and right side of the body.
- If absorbing energy, the energy flows from the Laogong to the chest and if toxins are being released, the toxins go through the chest and out through the Laogong.
- This meridian is for basic energy collecting and high-level energy boosting.

4. Wheel Meridian or WM (see figure 12)
   - This meridian is a forward-turning wheel within the abdomen, beginning in the area at the navel and ending in the area directly above the pubic bone.
   - The meridian touches the front and back walls inside of the abdomen.
   - This meridian is for transforming basic energy to middle-level energy.

Figure 12.

This figure shows the wheel meridian (aka WM)

5. Spiral Meridian or SM (see figures 13 and 14)
    *   This meridian is a clockwise turning spiral located within the abdomen, beginning in the area at the navel and ending in the area directly above the pubic bone.
    *   This meridian touches the side walls inside of the abdomen.
    *   This meridian is for transforming basic-level energy to middle-level energy.

Figure 13.

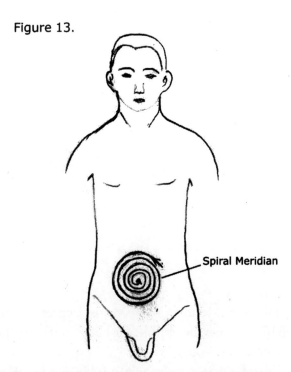

Spiral Meridian

This shows the location of the Spiral Meridian
(aka SM) in a Counterclockwise direction.

Figure 14.

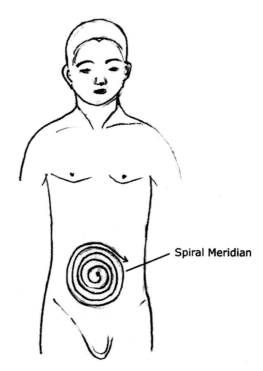

Spiral Meridian

This shows the Spiral Meridian (aka SM) in a Clockwise direction.

6. Vertical Spiral Meridian or VSM (see figures 15 and 16)
   - This meridian lies within the body, in the area between the Dantian and the clavicle.
   - This meridian is to stabilize middle-level energy.

Figure 15.

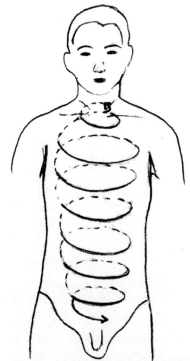

This figure shows the Vertical Spiral
Meridian (counterclockwise direction).

Figure 16.

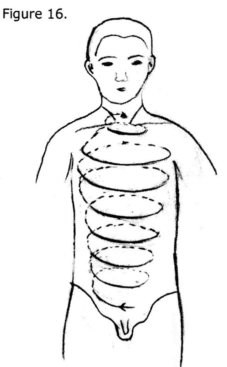

**This figure shows the Vertical Spiral Meridian
(clockwise direction)**

7. RN Meridian (see figure 17)
    • The RN Meridian begins at Huiying or RN1 and goes straight up through the middle of the chest between the breasts and continues upward, ending in the area underneath the bottom lip.
    • This meridian is for transforming middle-level energy to high-level energy.

Figure 17.

This figure shows the RN meridian.

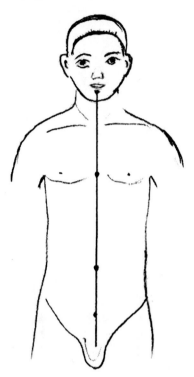

8. DU Meridian (see figure 18)
   • This meridian begins from the end of the tailbone, goes up along the spine, past the Mingmen or DU4, and continues up to DU20. The DU meridian then comes down the middle of the forehead, going past the middle of the nose, and ends in the area above the upper lip.
   • This meridian is for transforming middle-level energy to high-level energy.

Figure 18.

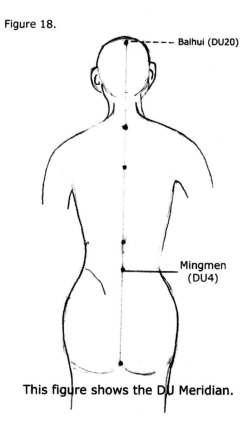

Baihui (DU20)

Mingmen (DU4)

This figure shows the DU Meridian.

9. Arm Yin Meridians (see figure 19)
   - There are three meridians, one of which is Pericardium Meridian or PCM.
   - These meridians start from the chest, ascend diagonally to the area between the under arm and shoulder, and descend through the arm, with PCM going down the middle of the arm and the other two meridians on either side. The two side meridians continue past the wrist and end at the tip of both the pinky finger and the thumb.
   - These meridians are used to raise energy from middle-level to high-level.

Figure 19.

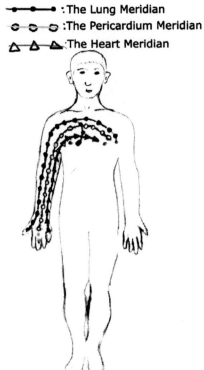

●━━●━━● : The Lung Meridian

◎━◎━◎ : The Pericardium Meridian

△━△━△ : The Heart Meridian

This figure shows the Arm Yin Meridians.

10. Arm Yang Meridians (see figure 20)

- There are three meridians beginning in the tips of the fingers—specifically the pinky, middle finger, and thumb. The meridians move through the hands, past the wrist, up the surface of the arm, and past the shoulders. The meridian continues to move up the side of the neck, past the side of the head, across to DU20, and finally, moves down the face.

- These meridians are used to raise energy from middle-level to high-level.

Figure 20.

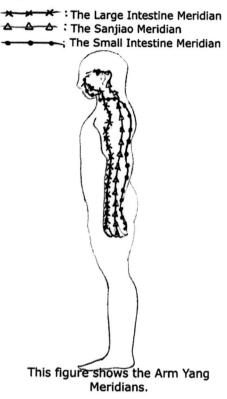

✕—✕—✕ : The Large Intestine Meridian
△—△—△ : The Sanjiao Meridian
●—●—● : The Small Intestine Meridian

This figure shows the Arm Yang Meridians.

11. Leg Yang Meridians (see figure 21)
   - Three meridians beginning in the face, moving to the side of the head and down the side of the neck, covering an area stretching from the side of the back and the side of body. These meridians continue to move down past the hip area and sacrum, through the side and back of the legs and end at the tips of the toes.
   - These meridians are used to raise energy from middle-level to high-level.

Figure 21.

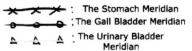

—✕—✕—✕— : The Stomach Meridian
—○—○—○— : The Gall Bladder Meridian
⬧   ⬧   ⬧ : The Urinary Bladder
                        Meridian

**This figure shows the Leg Yang
Meridians.**

12. Leg Yin Meridians (see figure 22)

- There are three meridians, one of which is the Kidney
  Meridian or KIM. Two of the meridians begin at the
  big toe, with KIM starting at the soles as was previously
  mentioned. The meridians go up the interior of the leg,
  continuing up to the Dantian, and separately travel up to
  the chest area.

- These meridians are used to raise energy from middle-level
  to high-level.

Figure 22.

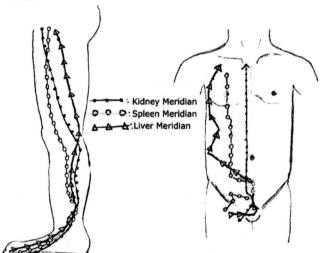

: Kidney Meridian
: Spleen Meridian
:Liver Meridian

This figure shows the Leg Yin Meridians.

MERIDIAN MEDITATION LEVELS

THERE ARE FIVE LEVELS for practicing Meridian Meditation: Beginner, Intermediate I, Intermediate II, Expert, and Master. Below will be a description of each.

Beginner (A minimum of one month): The beginner is learning to become quiet and relaxed, stop thinking, and keep the mind still. When you are a beginner, you do not get any major illnesses, but may occasionally experience minor illnesses, such as the flu. The beginner will learn how to breathe properly and which posture works best for them. The beginner will learn to identify and locate the points and meridians within the body.

Intermediate I (Four months): Those who practice on this intermediate level will learn how to collect energy from nature and absorb it into the body. Those on this level will also learn how to absorb energy into the Central Axis, Kidney, and Pericardium Meridians, and mix the energies within the Dantian area. They will also learn how filter toxins out of their bodies through these meridians. This level teaches how to recognize normal response from the practice. Those who are healthy and practice Meridian Meditation on this intermediate level notice a feeling of well-being and begin to notice higher levels of energy than they had previously, and if they are sick, those diseases will begin to partially heal.

Intermediate II (Six months): Those practicing on this intermediate level will learn how to utilize their Wheel, Spiral, and Vertical Spiral Meridians to help boost their energy levels. Those on this level will also learn to recognize and deal with abnormal responses from the practice of Meridian Meditation. When healthy people practice at this level, they will not get sick and have high-energy levels. Those who are sick and are practicing at this level feel a vast improvement.

Expert (a minimum of six months): Experts will begin to use their RN and DU Meridians to make one-cycle energy (see figure 30) and two-cycle energy (see figure 31) along with the Central Axis Meridian. Practicing at the expert level helps to improve memory. Those that are healthy practicing on the expert level always feel energetic and develop a very strong immune system, so they never get sick. Sick people practicing at the expert level have almost fully recovered from their illness.

Master (six months): When Meridian Meditation is practiced at this level, there is a free flow of energy through the twelve meridians. Masters develop super strength, have keen senses and powerful immune systems, and never develop illness.

PREPARATION

THE FOLLOWING IS A checklist of things one must do to prepare their body for the practice of Meridian Meditation.

- Wear loose-fitting clothes
- NO hats or headwear
- Remove all jewelry and watches
- Do not starve yourself prior to the meditation practice
- Make sure to eat a light meal, as you cannot practice on a full stomach
- No sexual intercourse should take place before practicing
- No alcohol should be consumed prior to practicing Meridian Meditation
- No more than one cup of coffee or tea before beginning to practice
- Pay attention to the time! As previously discussed, there are only certain times of the day that Meridian Meditation can be practiced
- Do not practice if you are in a very emotional state (ex. after an argument)

WARNINGS AND SUGGESTIONS

- You must begin Meridian Meditation at the Beginner's level
- No other meditative practices should be performed when one chooses to begin practicing Meridian Meditation
- Meridian Meditation, if practicing with others around, should only be performed in the presence of those who share your gender
- Once you begin the Intermediate I level, you must abstain from sexual intercourse for the first 100 days
- Those who regularly release energy through sexual intercourse have a much more difficult time feeling energy collection starting in the Dantian. It is necessary to take Qi and blood-toning herbal formula to enhance and support the current Qi or energy present.
- Never hold in urine or waste prior, during or after the practice
- Never practice Meridian Meditation when there is a thunderstorm or lightning present
- If practicing in the winter or in cold weather, you should make sure to dress warmly
- At any level, women should not practice once their menstrual cycle has begun

- One should cease smoking or drinking when looking to begin practicing Meridian Meditation
- During the practice of Meridian Meditation, one must not take any prescription drugs. These will interfere with the mediation and block the meridians, causing poor results.

HOW TO PRACTICE MERIDIAN MEDITATION

Beginner:

FIND A QUIET SPOT in nature and choose the posture you would like to use. Close your eyes, relaxing the eye muscles. Try to tune out noise, but if this is difficult, you may opt to use earplugs. Begin to clear the mind and do not consciously think about anything. Evenly and deeply begin to inhale and exhale through your nose, not your mouth. There should not be any noise from your breath as you breathe. You should be breathing from your diaphragm, not your chest. Gradually, over time, try to slow your breathing. As you breathe, try to notice the smells from nature as they come to you. After a while, shift your focus to the Dantian area. Do this for at least one hour every day. If you practice in a designated Meridian Meditation area, you may have to practice for six hours a day. You should practice at this level for a minimum of one month. During the practice, you may change your posture if necessary. If at any time you find yourself distracted, bring your focus back to the Dantian.

Intermediate I:

Do each of the energy absorption practices for one month.

Energy absorption through Baihui (see figure 23)

- First, choose your practice time and then your posture. If you choose to stand, face north or south as the magnetic field in these directions assist you in the practice.
- Relax your body and do not tense any muscles. Slightly close your mouth and close your eyes. Begin to inhale and exhale, deeply and slowly, from your diaphragm making sure to breathe through your nose. Focus your mind on the Dantian for three minutes, and then begin to practice. As you inhale, visualize golden energy from the sky (sun, stars, moon, etc. depending on time of practice) entering through the Baihui and going down through the Central Axis Meridian, straight down to the Dantian. At the end of the inhale, visualize the energy expanding to different directions of the lower abdomen. When you exhale, visualize the toxins in your body exiting the Dantian, going down through the Kidney Meridian, and leaving the body through the Yongquan or KI1. If this is done smoothly, you should notice that once you are finished with your visualization, your anus will contract twice on the inhale. At this point, begin to exhale.
- If you choose to sit, instead of visualizing the toxins exiting through the Yongquan, visualize the toxins moving upwards and exiting through the area in the chest just below the ribcage.

Figure 23.

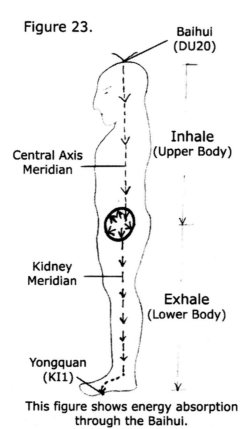

Baihui
(DU20)

Central Axis
Meridian

Inhale
(Upper Body)

Kidney
Meridian

Exhale
(Lower Body)

Yongquan
(KI1)

This figure shows energy absorption
through the Baihui.

- You should practice for at least half an hour for the first few days and gradually increase the amount of time.

- For men: If you would like to stop the meditation, keep your eyes closed and place the center of your left palm (PC8) on your belly button with your right over top. Move your hands in a circle clockwise 18 times, gradually making the circle bigger each time, and then move your hands counterclockwise 18 times, making the circle smaller each time. Count the circles in your head, not aloud.

- For women: To stop the meditation practice, put the center of your right palm (PC8) on your belly button and the left hand over top of the right. Move your hands counterclockwise 18 times, making the circle bigger each time, and then move your hands clockwise 18 times, making the circle smaller each time. Keep your eyes closed and do not count aloud.

- Once finished with the circles, both men and women must, with eyes still closed, take both hands and run them through the hair 12 times, going up from the forehead to the base of the head. Then, run hands through the sides of the hair 12 times starting at your temples. Next, take the fingers and run them across your face from the forehead, moving sideways to the temples. After that, massage the face starting from the middle of the forehead, down the sides of the nose, and sideways across the cheeks 12 times. Pull the tops of the ears outwards 12 times. Clench and release teeth 12 times. You may now end the meditation practice.
- You should practice at this level for one to two months.
- Normal responses for this level: At this level, you will normally notice a hot and/or cold feeling, some numbness, slight muscle spasms, mild skin irritation, pressure on certain points in the body or lightness in the body, crawling sensation along the meridians, much more gas release than normal, gurgling in the stomach, more saliva than normal, and a clearer mind.

Energy absorption through five points (see figure 24)

- The standing posture works best for this.
- Relax your muscles, close your eyes, and focus on the Dantian. Inhale and exhale slowly and deeply from your diaphragm and through your nose without any noise. Do this for five minutes. Begin to visualize that golden energy from the sky enters the Baihui or DU20, travels through the Central Axis Meridian, and goes to the Dantian. At the same time, golden energy from the air enters through your Laogong or PC8, travels through the Pericardium (PCM), goes to the chest area, and then straight down to the Dantian. Golden energy also enters from the Earth through the KI1 and travels through the Kidney Meridian or KIM and up to the Dantian.

- All the energy brought in through these five points should reach the Dantian at the same time. As you exhale, visualize toxins from the Dantian exiting through those same meridians and five points.

Figure 24.

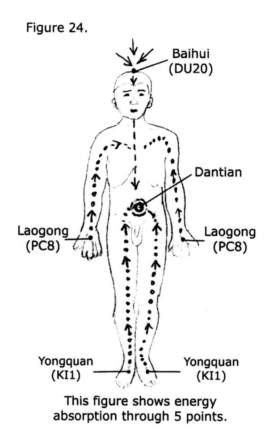

This figure shows energy
absorption through 5 points.

- Practice this for at least half an hour a day for the first few days and gradually increase.
- If you practice in a Meridian Meditation area, you usually will start out practicing for a few hours, even at the beginning.
- For men: If you would like to stop the meditation, keep your eyes closed and place the center of your left palm (PC8) on your belly button with your right over top. Move your hands in a circle clockwise 18 times, gradually making the circle bigger each time, and then move your hands counterclockwise 18

times, making the circle smaller each time. Count the circles in your head, not aloud.

- For women: To stop the meditation practice, put the center of your right palm (PC8) on your belly button and the left hand over top of the right. Move your hands counterclockwise 18 times, making the circle bigger each time, and then move your hands clockwise 18 times, making the circle smaller each time. Keep your eyes closed and do not count aloud.

- Once finished with the circles, both men and women must, with eyes still closed, take both hands and run them through the hair 12 times, going up from the forehead to the base of the head. Then, run hands through the sides of the hair 12 times starting at your temples. Next, take the fingers and run them across your face from the forehead, moving sideways to the temples. After that, massage the face starting from the middle of the forehead, down the sides of the nose, and sideways across the cheeks 12 times. Pull the top of the ears outwards 12 times. Clench and release teeth 12 times. You may now end the Meditation practice.

- Normal responses for this level of practice: A hot and/or cold feeling in the points, heaviness in the points, spasms and numbness in the points, crawling sensations at the point locations and more gas than normal. The whole body feels light and usually, after going to a spa or hot spring, there is a general feeling of wellness.

Intermediate II:

In order to practice at the Intermediate II level, you must complete Intermediate Level I. After Intermediate I, you can usually feel a ball in your lower tummy in the Dantian area. You should have a higher level of energy and be in a good mood, and you should also sleep soundly, have a good appetite, and experience regular bowel movements and urination patterns after completing Intermediate Level I.

Raising Energy I (see figure 25)

- The main focus of Raising Energy I, is working with the Wheel Meridian (WM).
- The posture recommended for this practice is sitting; however, you may also lie down. Take care to not fall asleep during the practice.
- Close your eyes, relax, and focus on the Dantian. Breathe through the nose, slowly and deeply, using your diaphragm for three to five minutes. When you inhale, imagine the Wheel Meridian (WM) begins to turn forward half-way, and as you exhale, it turns the rest of the way, completing the circle. The pace of the turn should match up with your breath. As it turns forward on the inhale, the WM should touch the front inner wall of the abdomen and on the exhale, the WM should touch the inner wall of your lower back.

Figure 25.

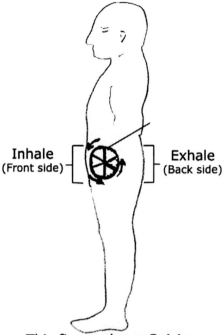

Inhale
(Front side)

Exhale
(Back side)

**This figure shows Raising
Energy I, working with the
Wheel Meridian.**

- Practice for at least half an hour for a few days and gradually increase to a few hours a day for one to two months.
- For men: If you would like to stop the meditation, keep your eyes closed and place the center of your left palm (PC8) on your belly button with your right over top. Move your hands in a circle clockwise 18 times, gradually making the circle bigger each time, and then move your hands counterclockwise 18 times, making the circle smaller each time. Count the circles in your head, not aloud.
- For women: To stop the meditation practice, put the center of your right palm (PC8) on your belly button and the left hand over top of the right. Move your hands counterclockwise 18 times, making the circle bigger each time, and then move your

hands clockwise 18 times, making the circle smaller each time. Keep your eyes closed and do not count aloud.

- Once finished with the circles, both men and women must, with eyes still closed, take both hands and run them through the hair 12 times, going up from the forehead to the base of the head. Then, run hands through the sides of the hair 12 times starting at your temples. Next, take the fingers and run them across your face from the forehead, moving sideways to the temples. After that, massage the face starting from the middle of the forehead, down the sides of the nose, and sideways across the cheeks 12 times. Pull the tops of the ears outwards 12 times. Clench and release teeth 12 times. You may now end the meditation practice.

- Normal responses that may be felt after practicing at this level are: strong sexual desire; for men, involuntary erections; feeling hot with a strong resistance to cold; feeling very energetic.

Raising Energy II (see figures 26 and 27)

- The main focus of Raising Energy II is working with the Spiral Meridian (SM).
- The navel or the bellybutton is the center of the Spiral Meridian.
- The posture recommended for this practice is sitting; however, you may also lie down. Take care to not fall asleep during the practice.
- Close your eyes, relax, and focus on the Dantian. Breath through the nose, slowly and deeply, using your diaphragm for three to five minutes. As you inhale, focus on the right side of the Spiral Meridian (SM), visualizing the spiral turning clockwise halfway. As you exhale, visualize it turning clockwise the rest of the way, ending with your focus on the right side of the SM.

Figure 26.

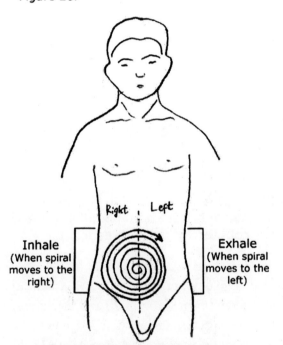

Right | Left

Inhale
(When spiral
moves to the
right)

Exhale
(When spiral
moves to the
left)

This figure shows Raising II Energy,
working with the Spiral Meridian (in
a clockwise direction)

Figure 27.

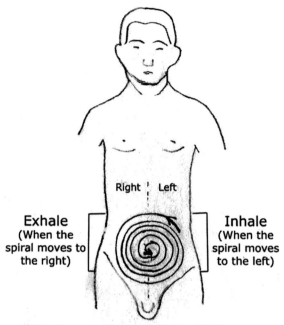

This figure shows Raising II Energy, working with the Spiral Meridian (in a counterclockwise direction.)

- For the first two days, practice your SM visualization 18 times in a row (it should turn like a spiral) and then visualize the same thing, but turning counterclockwise 18 times and shifting your focus from right to left of the SM. Begin with 18 times each way and gradually increase amount over time (36 times, 72 times, etc.) As you increase how many times you turn the spiral, the spiral will grow and gradually get bigger. The spiral should grow from the middle of the abdomen to just above the pubic bone.
- For men: If you would like to stop the meditation, keep your eyes closed and place the center of your left palm (PC8) on your belly button with your right over top. Move your hands in a circle clockwise 18 times, gradually making the circle bigger each time, and then move your hands counterclockwise 18

times, making the circle smaller each time. Count the circles in your head, not aloud.

- For women: To stop the meditation practice, put the center of your right palm (PC8) on your belly button and the left hand over top of the right. Move your hands counterclockwise 18 times, making the circle bigger each time, and then move your hands clockwise 18 times, making the circle smaller each time. Keep your eyes closed and do not count aloud.

- Once finished with the circles, both men and women must, with eyes still closed, take both hands and run them through the hair 12 times, going up from the forehead to the base of the head. Then, run hands through the sides of the hair 12 times starting at your temples. Next, take the fingers and run them across your face from the forehead, moving sideways to the temples. After that, massage the face starting from the middle of the forehead, down the sides of the nose, and sideways across the cheeks 12 times. Pull the tops of the ears outwards 12 times. Clench and release teeth 12 times. You may now end the meditation practice.

- Normal responses for this level of practice are: there is less gas production, you begin to feel a reduction in the size of the Dantian.

Raising Energy III (see figures 28 and 29)

- The main focus of Raising Energy III is learning to work with the Vertical Spiral Meridian (VSM).
- At this level, energy begins to rise up through the stomach and the chest. It is at this level that we begin to see both normal and abnormal responses.
- The posture recommended for this practice is standing.
- Close your eyes, relax, and focus on the Dantian. Breath through the nose, slowly and deeply, using your diaphragm for three to five minutes. Begin to visualize golden energy circling upwards vertically starting from the Dantian, up through the chest, and ending in the clavicle area. On the inhale, circle the

energy clockwise halfway and on the exhale, circle the energy the rest of the way to complete the spiral.

- On the inhale turn, the spiral should touch the inner front walls of your body (abdominal or chest side) and on the exhale, the spiral should touch the inner back walls of your body.
- After visualizing this, begin to visualize the golden energy circling downwards vertically, starting from the clavicle area and ending in the Dantian. On the inhale, circle the energy counterclockwise halfway and on the exhale, circle the energy counterclockwise the rest of the way to complete the spiral.
- On the inhale turn, the spiral should touch the inner back walls of your body and on the exhale turn, the spiral should touch the inner front walls of your body.
- The spiral should always be smaller in the abdominal area and bigger in the chest area.
- The pace of the spiral should match with your breathing.

Figure 28.

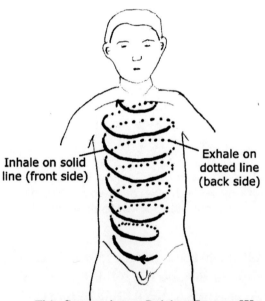

Inhale on solid line (front side)

Exhale on dotted line (back side)

This figure shows Raising Energy III,
working with the Vertical Spiral Meridian
(in a clockwise direction).

Figure 29.

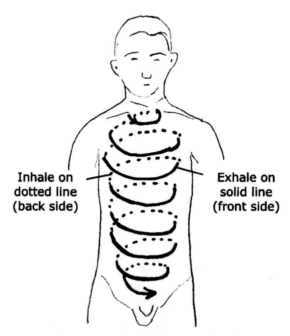

Inhale on
dotted line
(back side)

Exhale on
solid line
(front side)

**This figure shows Raising Energy III,
working with the Vertical Spiral Meridian
(in a counterclockwise direction)**

- If you feel at any point that the spiral is stuck and you cannot move it any further, do not try to force it. Instead, stop and return to the previous two Raising Energy levels.
- Make sure to move the spiral correctly or you may get an abnormal response.
- You should move the spiral up and then down and repeat this 72 times.
- For men: If you would like to stop the meditation, keep your eyes closed and place the center of your left palm (PC8) on your belly button with your right over top. Move your hands in a circle clockwise 18 times, gradually making the circle bigger each time, and then move your hands counterclockwise 18 times, making the circle smaller each time. Count the circles in your head, not aloud.

- For women: To stop the meditation practice, put the center of your right palm (PC8) on your belly button and the left hand over top of the right. Move your hands counterclockwise 18 times, making the circle bigger each time, and then move your hands clockwise 18 times, making the circle smaller each time. Keep your eyes closed and do not count aloud.
- Once finished with the circles, both men and women must, with eyes still closed, take both hands and run them through the hair 12 times, going up from the forehead to the base of the head. Then, run hands through the sides of the hair 12 times starting at your temples. Next, take the fingers and run them across your face from the forehead, moving sideways to the temples. After that, massage the face starting from the middle of the forehead, down the sides of the nose, and sideways across the cheeks 12 times. Pull the tops of the ears outwards 12 times. Clench and release teeth 12 times. You may now end the meditation practice.
- Raising Energy III should be practiced for over two months.
- Normal responses for this level of practice: most will feel a heavy, solid feeling in the Dantian area and will also feel expansion in this area; the Baihui, Yongquan, Laogong and Mingmen points will all feel very hot; most will feel a muscle spasm around the Huiying; most will also feel extremely energetic and never get tired.
- Abnormal responses for this level of practice: Headaches.
- If experiencing headaches, do not take painkillers. The best way to deal with the headaches is to press on KI1.

Expert:

It is very important to complete the previous levels in order to develop enough chi (energy) to practice at this level, otherwise, it is very likely that abnormal response will occur.

Level I

One-Cycle Energy through RN-DU Meridians (see figure 30)

- The main focus of Expert level I is to work with the RN and DU Meridians.
- Usually, if the previous levels are practiced correctly and efficiently, energy levels should be high enough to flow into these two meridians.
- Those who do not feel energy flowing into these two meridians should go back to previous levels and practice more.
- Those who feel energy in these two meridians, but the energy does not flow smoothly, should practice working with these meridians more. Increase practice time and use a different posture.
- When practicing, the sitting and standing postures are recommended.
- Begin breathing. Inhale and visualize that energy from the Dantian area moves down, past the Huiying, and then moves up through the meridians up to the DU20.
- Exhale and visualize the energy moving from the DU20 back down to the Dantian.
- You should feel an intense, warm sensation move quickly from the Huiying up the spine during the practice.
- The energy should move automatically as you visualize and if it does, you have successfully achieved energy flow in the RN and DU Meridians.
- Some successfully achieve energy flow in these two meridians, but stress, sex or other factors cause a reduction in energy levels. If this happens, you should return to the previous levels of practice to increase energy levels and energy flow.

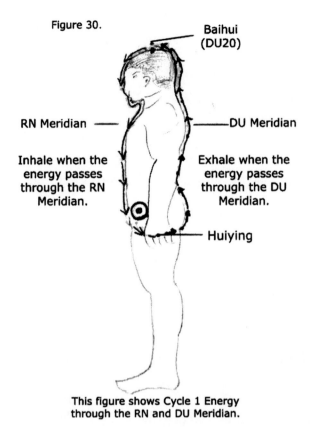

Figure 30.

Baihui
(DU20)

RN Meridian ——

——DU Meridian

Inhale when the
energy passes
through the RN
Meridian.

Exhale when the
energy passes
through the DU
Meridian.

—— Huiying

This figure shows Cycle 1 Energy
through the RN and DU Meridian.

- Unlike the previous levels, there is no need to complete the exercise to stop meditation when practicing on this level.
- The amount of time you should practice at this level for will vary between those who practice, but you will know once you have successfully completed this level based on your body's response. On average, completion of this level takes 2-6 months.
- Normal responses for this level of practice: the point between your eyebrows feels much lighter; it also feels like there is a small, burning ball in this area; it will feel like very warm water is flowing through the RN and DU Meridians; the mind is very clear and still; the body feels very light, almost like you are floating.

- Abnormal responses for this level of practice: headaches, confusion, anxiety, worry, and trembling.
- If you have an abnormal response, you should go back to previous levels as your body's energy levels are not yet high enough to practice at this level.

Level II

Two-Cycle Energy through RN, DU, and Central Axis Meridians (see figure 31)

- The main focus of Expert level II is not only to continue to focus on and work with the RN and DU Meridians, but also to focus on and work with the Central Axis Meridian (DU20) as well.
- Sitting or standing is the recommended postures for this level of practice.
- Breathe deeply and relax the whole body for three minutes and then begin to practice.
- When you inhale, imagine energy begins in the Huiying, moving upwards through the RN and DU Meridians up to the DU20.
- When you exhale, imagine energy going from the DU20 back down the Central Axis Meridian, through the Dantian and continuing further down to the Huiying.

Figure 31.

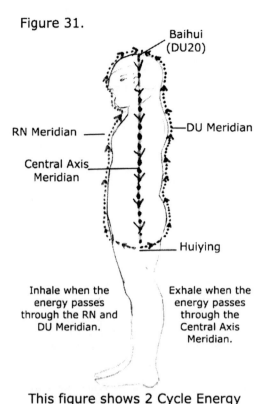

Baihui
(DU20)

RN Meridian

DU Meridian

Central Axis
Meridian

Huiying

Inhale when the
energy passes
through the RN and
DU Meridian.

Exhale when the
energy passes
through the
Central Axis
Meridian.

This figure shows 2 Cycle Energy
through the 3 Meridians.

- You should practice at this level for at least five months.
- The normal response to this level of practice is the same as in Expert Level I.
- Usually, if Level I is successfully completed, you will not get an abnormal response when practicing at this level.

Master:

- This level focuses on the Leg Yin, Arm Yin, Arm Yang, and Leg Yang Meridians (see figures 22, 19, 20, and 21).
- The standing posture is best for this level, though, all postures can be used.
- Before you begin to practice, you need to do some deep breathing for three minutes.

- When breathing in, visualize energy moving from the Dantian, through the Kidney Meridian and down to the KI1. Now exhale.
- Do not visualize the energy moving back up; just keep visualizing the energy moving from the Dantian to the KI1 for three minutes.
- After three minutes, on the inhale, imagine energy flowing from the KI1 through the Leg Yin Meridians, moving upwards to the Huiying, continuing to the Dantian and expanding to the chest. On the exhale, imagine energy moving from the chest and through the Arm Yin Meridians on both sides of the body.
- On the next inhale, imagine the energy, beginning in the fingertips, moving through the Arm Yang Meridians and ending at the head. Now exhale and visualize the energy from the head moving down through the Leg Yang Meridians and ending at the feet.
- This is one complete cycle. Repeat all steps that you completed after the three-minute visualization and practice doing these cycles for at least one hour.
- When practicing, it is very easy for the body to move and not keep still. If your body begins to move, press the tip of your thumb and middle finger together using your left hand and press the tip of your thumb to the base of your ring finger on your left hand.
- If your energy levels are not high enough to practice at this level, it is very easy to get an abnormal response, such as confusion and trembling.
- You should practice at this level for at least six months.
- Once you successfully complete this level, you will never get sick again.

DISEASES THAT CAN BE EFFECTIVELY TREATED WITH MERIDIAN MEDITATION

MERIDIAN MEDITATION CAN HELP cure most illnesses. The positive effects this meditation can have on diseases have been confirmed by my university instructor, colleagues, and clients; even I have witnessed the wonderful effects of Meridian Meditation. The following is a list of diseases that Meridian Meditation can help with:

Cardiovascular System:

- Coronary heart diseases
- Preexisting cardiac infection
- Irregular heartbeat (ex. palpitations, racing heart, slow heart rate)
- Chronic myocarditis
- High or low blood pressure
- Heart murmur
- Rheumatic heart diseases

Digestive System:

- Peptic ulcer
- Gastro duodenal ulcer
- H. Pylori
- Chronic gastritis
- Gastroptosia
- GERD or acid reflux
- Colitis/chronic colitis/ulcerative colitis
- Intestinal colic
- Chronic cirrhosis of liver
- Chronic kidney disease
- Intestinal adhesion
- Constipation
- Diarrhea
- Irritable bowel syndrome
- Anorexia nervosa
- Dysentery

Respiratory System:

- Bronchiectasis
- Asthma
- Bronchitis
- Tuberculosis
- Pulmonary emphysema
- Flu
- Silicosis
- Pleurisy

Motor System:

- Rheumatoid arthritis
- Osteoarthritis
- Cervical spondylopathy
- Omarthritis
- Degenerative disk disorder

- Hernia
- Progressive myotrophy
- Progressive myodystrophy
- Back pain or lumbago
- Lumbosacral strain
- Soft tissue injury

Endocrine System:

- Hyperthyroidism
- Hypothyroidism
- Diabetes
- Obesity

Nervous System:

- Post-stroke
- Neurodermatitis or paralysis
- All anxiety disorders
- Insomnia
- Multiple sclerosis
- Parkinson's disease

Urinary/Reproductive System:

- Nephrotic syndrome
- Pyelonephritis
- Chronic nephritis
- Impotence
- Nocturnal emission
- Prospermia
- Endometriosis
- Irregular menstruation
- Menopause symptoms
- PMS
- Dysmenorrhea
- Chronic pelvic inflammation

- Fibrosis
- Urinary tract infections
- Dysfunction uterine bleeding
- Hyperplasia of mammary glands
- Neurosism

Sense System:

- Far-sighted or near-sighted vision
- Tinnitus
- Hearing loss
- Glaucoma
- Astigmatism
- Chronic rhinitis
- Chronic tonsillitis
- Toothaches
- Ulcer of the mouth
- Sinusitis
- Abscess tooth

Immune System:

- Low white blood cells
- Low NK cells
- Tumor

If you begin practicing Meridian Meditation with a poor nervous system or severe system diseases, it is much harder to see the results. Some examples of the diseases that would make it difficult to see results are:

- Schizophrenia
- Bipolar disorder
- Severe depression
- Acute infection (ex. pneumonia, hematosepsis, etc.)
- Severe bleeding

CONCLUSION: POWERFUL HOLISTIC HEALING

MERIDIAN MEDITATION IS THE safest and most effective treatment option for almost every possible health condition and if you are healthy, it can help keep you this way. Meridian Meditation is universal and anyone can practice and benefit regardless of age, gender, race or religion. It costs little to no money, and gives your body the opportunity to heal and revitalize itself, giving you a new lease on life.

Many people focus on the parts of the body as though they are separate from the whole; but they are not separate, they are in fact one system. This connection is why it is so important to treat the body as whole, rather than to treat the area that is not functioning as it should. Both Western medicine and alternative health practitioners often do not understand this and so, this fact is usually ignored when treating patients. Today there appears to be a heavy reliance on things, such as medications, to bring about good health and relieve pain, but the truth is that all practices have their imperfections. Chinese herbal medicine relies on intellect and knowledge to diagnose a health issue, and this leaves an ample amount of room for a patient to be misdiagnosed. Acupuncture often cannot treat those who have depleted energy stores or energy deficiencies and Western medicine often prescribes medications that only mask the issue and target specific areas, causing the patient to only feel better temporarily. Most medications also have side effects that can be long lasting, causing the patient to suffer to a greater degree than they initially did and may even put patients at risk of death (ex. withdrawal).

It is hard for many people to understand Meridian Meditation due to the amount of trust and reliance on more traditional medicine, but we have the inherent ability to self-heal. Meridian Meditation can help uncover and strengthen this healing ability that is built into our bodies. A lot of people seem to believe that if they eat healthier, that that will be enough to boost energy, heal the body and mind, and ward off sickness, but this is false. Eating healthier foods is not enough as there are three sources that we need to derive energy from and spending time in nature is the most important. The human body, as we have discussed, is a holistic body. The human body is also a part of nature, perfectly attuning to the patterns of nature and easily absorbing energy from it. The energy from nature is extremely powerful and a very important source of energy for the body. We can take in this energy just from being outside and breathing in the air. Healthy foods can also help give us the right kind of energy since when it is fresh and natural, it is free from the toxins and additives that are usually added to the food we have available today, and finally, we have our own natural inborn energy stores. These three sources of energy mix together, synthesis and flow to every area of our body when we practice Meridian Meditation, integrating body and mind, keeping us happy, healthy and energized.

REFERENCES

Wendan Mo, *The Secret of Qigong(Chinese)*, China, *Guangxi Science and Technology Publishing Co. 1989.*

Xiuyuan Chen, *Yellow Emperor-Ling And Su Annotation(Chinese), China, Haihuiwen Press, 1865*

Jizhou Yang, *Acupuncture Dacheng(Chinese), China, People's health publisher, 1963*

Lu Zhang, *Zhang Tong Medicine(Chinese), China, Classical Medical publisher, 1695,*

Pumi Huang, *Acupuncture and B by(Chines), Chiina, People's Health publisher, 1996*

Zhichao, Chinese Excellent Qigong(Chinese), China, Chinese Esperanto Publisher, 1994

Mingwu Zhang, Chinese Qigong Therapy, China, Shandong Science and Technology press, 1988

Tianbin Song, TCM Qigong(Chinese), China, Chinese TCM publisher, 1994

CPSIA information can be obtained at www.ICGtesting.com
Printed in the USA
LVOW11s0535161014

408748LV00004B/9/P